A Girl Named Carrie

Cover. Portrait of Carrie Neiman.

Page 2-3. Carrie Neiman with (left to right) Mrs. Dulany Lingo, Miss J. A. Humphrey, Mrs. Angus Wynne, Jr., Miss Nancy Ann Smith, Mrs.Dudley Ramdsden, Mrs. Fred Schoellkopf, Jr. Photograph by Thomas Benton Hollyman, Holiday Magazine, March 1953.

Page 4-5. Photograph of a model standing in the jewelry section of the downtown Dallas Neiman-Marcus store.

Page 10. Jerrie Marcus, at bottom right, talks to her parents, grandparents, aunts, and uncles during a Sunday lunch in her grandparent's backyard, on Oakwood Lane in Dallas, Texas. Photograph by Nina Leen / Getty.

Page 12. A detail of lace selected from the V&A by Carrie Neiman for Jo Cherry Holman's 1948 wedding dress. photograph by Allison V. Smith.

Page 14-15. Mrs.Neiman, Miss Cullen buying gowns at Nettie Rosenstein's in New York.

Page 16-17. Neiman-Marcus window display.

Page 18. Contact sheet showing a model wearing a fur jacket and gloves. Photographs by John Rogers, ca. 1965.

Page 20. Letter to the author, Jerrie Marcus, from Aunt Carrie Neiman, on the day she was born.

Page 22-23. A photograph of Carrie Neiman's home on Swiss Avenue in Dallas Texas. Photographed by Allison V. Smith.

Library of Congress Control Number: 2021916584

Printed in the United States of America.

10   9   8   7   6   5   4   3   2   1

The paper used in this book meets the minimum requirements of the American National Standard for Permanence of Paper for Printed Library Materials, z39.48.1984. Binding materials have been chosen for durability.

Library of Congress Control Number: 2021916584

ISBN 978-0-578-96960-2 (cloth)

To Wendy Marcus Raymont

Who had planned to co-author
this family tale with me.
As a fine editor and exceptional
sister, she is greatly missed.

The Briscoe Center for American History, The University of Texas at Austin,
Texas Jewish Historical Society Records, 1824–2019

Valerie Steele, Director and Chief Curator of
The Museum at the Fashion Institute of Technology

Temple Emanu-El, Dallas, Anjelica Ruiz, Director of Libraries and Archives

Dallas Historical Society

DeGolyer Library Southern Methodist University,
Russell Martin, Anne Peterson Terre Heydari and Christina Jensen

Flashback Dallas, Paula Bosse

Hillsboro Public Library, Russell Keelin

Victoria and Albert Museum Archives, Textiles

M. S. Siddy Rosenberg, Archive Manager, Heather Johnson and Staff,
The Temple-Congregation Adath Israel Brith Sholom, Louisville, Kentucky

Texas Christian University, Linda Chenoweth,
Jeff Bond, Laura Steinbach, Mary Couts Burnett Library,

Fort Worth Public Library, Kathryn King

City of Dallas Public Library, Mary Jo Giudice and Christine Sharbrough

Amon Carter Museum of American Art, Jonathan Frembling, Archivist

Lakewood Country Club, Dallas, Ray De Tullio and Curt Sampson

Texas Jewish Historical Society and Jack Gerrick

University of North Texas Libraries

The Portal to Texas History, Jake Mangum, Ruby Raines,
Office of the President (Ret.)

Texas Fashion Collection, University of North Texas, Annette Becker, Director

Book designed by DJ Stout and Michaela Lehman
Pentagram, Austin, Texas

Acknowledgments

My deepest thanks go to many people, family and friends, who for years have patiently listened to me talk about Aunt Carrie and hear why she is so important. Of course, my father was a great source of information as well as was his younger brother, my Uncle Lawrie. So too were the many now retired sales people who shared their own personal memories. I am extremely grateful to Sarah Drake, a superb researcher who refused to leave any stone unturned. My daughter, Allison, a tireless photo editor, has dedicated her life to unearthing and preserving family photos, and I am grateful that she kept pushing me to get this done.

Thanks to my brother, Richard Marcus, my cousins Herb Marcus, Sarah Jacobus, Ann Folz, my cousin Raymond Garfield and his mother, Jean, who is my oldest living relative who just celebrated her 105th birthday. Thanks to Elizabeth Robertson for telling me the story of the exquisite lace Carrie found at the Victoria and Albert Museum in London. The lace was used in a wedding dress in 1943 and was photographed by Allison for the title page of this book. Thanks to Sandy Marple, a longtime Neiman Marcus employee, whose knowledge of The Store is immeasurable. Thanks to Fernando Alvarez Caraccioli, Evans Caglage, Michael Thomas and Barry Whistler for sharing their knowledge and skills, and to the best editors, Jane Wolfe, Nancy Visser, Dana Frank, and Bill Minutaglio. A final thanks to my friends Doris Kearns Goodwin and Rena Pederson, who over the years convinced me to tell Carrie's story.

Foreword

Aunt Carrie was always an impressive member of the
Marcus family. Growing up, I never understood why she was so
important. She just was. Even now, more than 70 years later,
friends will tell me stories they recall their mothers telling them
about their exciting trips to New York with Mrs. Neiman
to find the perfect wedding dress. Or stories about waiting in a
large fitting room on the second floor while Mrs. Neiman
searched through the storeroom to find the proper hat for the
proper suit. Or how exciting it was just to meet her. As I
have delved more deeply into Carrie's life, I finally began to see
what I had been missing in this regal woman with an innate
knowledge of style, perfection and compassion. She had, like my
Uncle Lawrie once said, "nerves of steel and a heart of butter."

A Girl Named Carrie

Jerrie Marcus Smith

WITH ALLISON V. SMITH

CAIRN PRESS, DALLAS, TEXAS

THE WOMEN WHO MOLD THE STOR

. . . buying gowns at Nettie Rosenstein's in New
Marcus in Dallas. Miss Cullen (right) virtually lives

STYLE: MRS. NEIMAN, MISS CULLEN

.. Rosenstein creations are exclusive with Neiman-
ew York; Mrs. Neiman goes there four times a year.

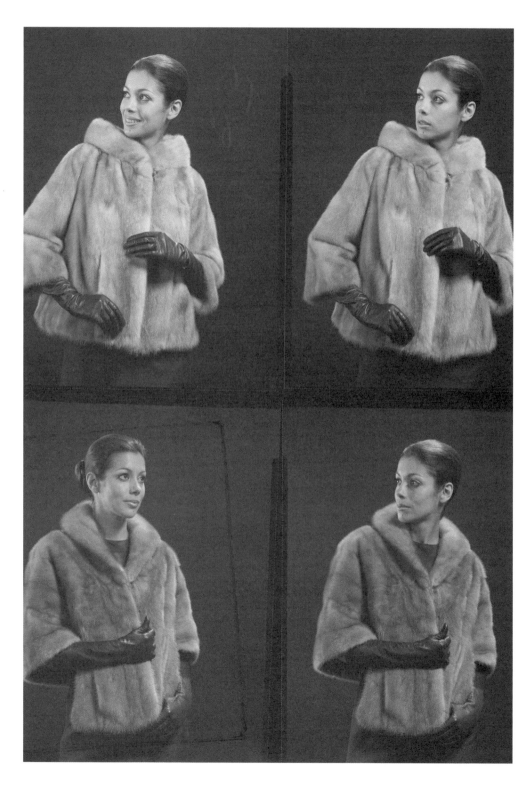

Contents

Sept 7th –

Dearest Jerry; I am so proud
of my new niece, and I
love her name – Aunt Minnie
and I can hardly wait to
see you –

We are so happy that your
mother is doing so well,
and send love and congratulations to both your mother
& Dad,

I am sending you a check, so your Dad can open a bank account for you, and hoping to add to same all the time so that when you are a big girl, you will be able to do some special things you will nodout want to do.

Lots of love and kisses to you and your mother & Dad,
Lovingly,
Aunt Carrie.

CHAPTER ONE

More Than I
Ever Imagined

I have long wondered about my mysterious great aunt Carrie Neiman.

When I was young, Aunt Carrie struck me as a brooding, humorless relative — a very old, thin and somber-looking woman with dark circles under her eyes, always dressed in black, with pearls around her neck and two thick gold bracelets on her wrist. She was my grandfather's younger sister, divorced with no children, and she lived for years in Old East Dallas in an imposing three-story red-brick house on elegant Swiss Avenue.

In a way, the home echoed her demeanor. One of her great nephews, Herbert Marcus III, once described it as spooky, rather like a morgue. I remember it as an eerie, quiet and dark home with heavy silk curtains, always tightly drawn, and a multitude of overstuffed sofas and chairs in the living room, all of them stiff and uninviting for children. The heavy mahogany table in the formal dining room was always set for yet another serious family dinner, with ornate silver, crystal goblets of dark ruby red and the finest bone china.

My brother and sister saw it the same way: We dreaded visiting the house, especially going to the closed-in porch upstairs, where we were ushered every Sunday to pay our respects to our incapacitated and ancient cigar-smoking great uncle Abe. He and his wife, Carrie's older sister, Minnie, lived with Aunt Carrie, and he was cared for full time by a white-uniformed nurse. Years earlier Uncle Abe was injured when the boiler went out in the basement. He foolishly lit a match to locate the source of the gas and the boiler exploded, burning large areas of his body.

The house, and the people in it, seemed lonely and forbidding, but there was one wonderful escape — a tall, narrow toy closet on the second floor. We children would race to it and explore its treasure of delightful toys, books and dolls — all things Carrie had collected on her frequent buying trips to Europe — anything to keep us from the earnest discussions among the adults. In Aunt Carrie's house, we knew that young children were to be seen and not heard.

Page 24. A portrait of Carrie Marcus Neiman.

Page 27. Interior of Carrie Neiman's dining room in her Swiss Avenue home in Dallas, Texas.

When it was time for me to leave, I could see Aunt Carrie's shiny long black Packard in the driveway, awaiting her summons. There were times when I got to ride in it — it was always chauffeur-driven — but I would be told to sit in a jump seat, against my wishes, rather than on the upholstered bench with the adults.

Sometimes, in the hushed confines of the car, after leaving the big house with its treasure closet, I would wonder if there was more to Great Aunt Carrie than I ever imagined.

***

In 1953, when I was just 16, Aunt Carrie died of lung cancer. She passed away two months shy of her 70th birthday. I was just finishing high school and a typical self-absorbed teenager, to say the least: On the night she succumbed to cancer, I was upset because I had to give up going to my Hockaday School senior class costume party. My parents said that it wouldn't look right for me to be seen partying.

As time went on, I learned that Aunt Carrie was, in fact, adored and respected by many in the family and in the Store, Neiman Marcus. But for years, I knew her to be a deadly serious soul, someone who talked business nonstop and had nothing in common with me, a rather spoiled, selfish teenager.

I eventually learned that my early impressions of her were flat-out wrong. What I had missed out on, while talking on the telephone or hanging out with my friends, was getting to know the thoroughly modern business woman who was the quiet genius behind the success of the internationally famous emporium known as Neiman Marcus.

My great aunt, the stern-looking lady in the black dress who was visible daily in the Women's Department on the second floor, was busy guiding the global success of one of the best-known stores in the world.

Page 28-29. Interior of Carrie Neiman's living room in her Swiss Avenue home in Dallas, Texas.

Page 30. The author, Jerrie Marcus Smith, photographed in her father's library in her childhood home in Dallas. Photograph by Stanley Marcus, 1946.

Page 33. Jerrie Marcus (second from left), photographed with her siblings, Richard and Wendy Marcus, and her mother, Billie Marcus, in Cambridge, England. Photograph by Elsbeth Juda, 1948.

Excellence and Exceptionalism

C arrie Marcus was born on May 5, 1883, in Louisville, Kentucky, the fourth of five children of Jacob and Delia Bloomfield Marcus. Her parents were recently arrived Jewish immigrants from Wronke, Germany, a town on the German-Polish border. The children were a motley bunch. Theo, the oldest, was remembered by one nephew as "an awful lot of fun" and by another as grumpy and overweight. Herbert, the second oldest, was said to be forward thinking and progressive about most things, as well as a dreamer. The third in line, Minnie, was described as either a "dominating tyrant" or "dependent and shy." Celia, the youngest, won a beauty pageant at 16, then eloped the following year.

Carrie was 10 in 1893, when Jacob and Delia moved the family from the vibrant cultured city of Louisville to the dusty little town of Hillsboro, Texas, sixty miles southwest of Dallas. One of Jacob's cousins had prospered in Hillsboro, working with farmers as a cotton broker, or "cotton factor," as they were also known. Jacob hoped to make it as big as his cousin, and Texas seemed ripe with opportunity for a man with ambition.

Hillsboro had a population of 5,300 nearing the turn of the twentieth century. It was the county seat and the agricultural center of Hill County, which had 41,355 residents. A post office had been built in Hillsboro thirty years earlier, and *The Hillsboro Express* newspaper had been in publication since before the Civil War. Jacob presumably appreciated that there was a growing Jewish community in Hillsboro, to go along with plenty of cotton and several established gins and textile mills. There were some wealthy families in Hillsboro — almost all tied to cotton — and they lived in large newly built Victorian homes around the town square, many with a hitching post in front. Despite the handful of wealthy residents, the town had precious few cultural outlets, though, and life in Hillsboro was a big adjustment for the Marcuses, who loved literature, art and music.

As Jacob joined his cousin in the cotton business, his children were educated mostly at home. Jacob and Delia believed in a kind of Germanic excellence and exceptionalism. Unlike many families in Hillsboro, the Marcuses listened to classical music and read voraciously. Although they had little money, they began building a substantial library that included the classics of Western civilization. They devoured the latest news from Europe in the English and German newspapers that somehow found their way to the Texas hamlet. *The Spectator*, from London, was a favorite. At an early age, Carrie developed an interest in European-inspired art and fashion, influenced, in part, by her parents and by her constant reading of books, newspapers and magazines from Germany, France and England. While it is unclear whether the Marcuses regularly spoke German at home, Carrie was certainly able to read the German-language materials that came into the house.

Herbert, five years older than Carrie, was a restless teenager and he found work in a clothing store. But with no cultural institutions, Hillsboro in the evenings was often dull, and after four years there, he decided that small-town life was not for him. In 1899, determined to find a more cultured city, Herbert left for the big town to the north — Dallas.

With a population of 38,000 in 1900, Dallas was seven times larger than Hillsboro, but it was hardly a metropolis. As in Hillsboro, many of the principal streets in Dallas were unpaved and transportation was by horse-drawn carriage or cart, both of which had to fight for the right of way with trains that crisscrossed downtown Dallas. There were forty-six saloons on Elm Street (where Neiman Marcus would eventually open), and with men stumbling in and out of them at lunchtime, the city could be a rough place for a single woman. In parts of downtown, it was said that a woman seen walking alone on the city's streets even in daylight was not considered a lady. The promoters of a new subdivision called Highland

ET SCENE, HILLSBORO, TEX.

WAUKEE, NO. 5399

Park claimed that downtown Dallas was nothing but "business houses, saloons, dust and heat."

Yet Dallas was beginning to show some signs of sophistication. It already had its Red Book, which its publisher claimed was the first register of "high society" in the state of Texas. The city also had a symphony orchestra and an opera company, and it boasted a Shakespeare Club. Dallas was clearly a city on the rise, a big step up from the little town that Herbert had left behind.

Soon after arriving in Dallas, Herbert found a job as a shoe salesman at Sanger Brothers, which, according to Leon Harris's 1979 book *Merchant Princes*, was "the greatest dry goods company west of the Mississippi." Although Herbert had not completed college, much less grade school or high school, he excelled at selling shoes and interacting with customers throughout the store. Sanger Brothers' extraordinarily successful owner, Philip Sanger, recognized Herbert's strong ambition and his phenomenal work ethic, and soon he promoted Herbert to buyer of boys' clothing. Despite, or perhaps because of, his humble upbringing, Herbert quickly developed expensive tastes, especially in clothes. Investing virtually all of his earnings in his wardrobe, he wore the finest suits and shoes, while bringing his lunch to work, carried in a brown paper bag.

Carrie, still a teenager living in Hillsboro, was anxious to join her older sibling in Dallas but first had to convince her parents to let her go, which was not easy. They worried that she would be a financial burden on Herbert. But, after much effort, she convinced them that she would find a job and support herself. In 1901, she moved to Dallas and immediately went to work at a specialty store called A. Harris & Co., which had been founded fourteen years earlier, in 1887. She was put in charge of selling women's blouses, earning $10 a week (about $300 a week in 2020 dollars).

At the age of 18, Carrie displayed charm, impeccable manners and a desire to learn, qualities that helped her do well in the brand-new business of selling ready-to-wear clothes. While working on the salesfloor, she learned that there was an art to making customers feel special, and she was determined to excel at it. She gave each customer personal attention, a skill that she would hone and develop for years to come — to the point that she would be unsurpassed in American retailing during the first half of the twentieth century.

Carrie, wise beyond her years, wanted financial independence when she moved to Dallas, and she found it, even managing to save a little money. Like her brother Herbert, who was quickly promoted at Sanger Brothers, Carrie advanced at A. Harris to a position as a buyer for the women's blouse department. Drawing on her knowledge of fashion from Paris and Germany, garnered from her consumption of European newspapers and magazines, Carrie displayed extraordinary self-confidence and an impressive sense of style. She was not afraid to purchase clothing and goods that were vastly different from what other Dallas stores were offering. Instead of

MR. AND MRS. A. L. NEIMAN.

NEIMAN-MARCUS WEDDING

'Twas in Youth's fair, immortal spring,
When Cupid rallied in the ring—
Rare choice of weapons love affords—
Some fight with arrows, some with
    swords;
And one before the god has knelt
With just a Carrie at his belt.

A recent battle has been fought,
And two young hearts are safely
    caught.
With laughter shining in his eyes,
Love brings to Hymen's Court his prize,
The blushing captives greet their king,
And Hymen binds them with a ring.
          —O. P. S.

From Dallas comes the echoes of a
pretty home wedding, which was sol-
emnized last Tuesday evening, in
which Mr. A. L. Neiman of this city
and Miss Carrie Marcus of Dallas were
the central figures.

Miss Marcus is the youngest daughter of Mr. and Mrs. Jacob Marcus of
144 Marion street, Dallas, where she
numbers her friends by the hundreds,
she having been a prime favorite since
making her debut in Dallas society.
Mr. Neiman, formerly of Chicago, is
manager of the American Salvage
Company's southwestern office, which
is located in this city. While a resi-
dent of Fort Worth less than a year,
he has made a reputation as a bril-
liant and honorable young business
man.

The wedding, although a quiet home
affair, with only the relatives of the
contracting parties present, was one
of the prettiest seen in Dallas in many
a day.

The interior of the Marcus home in
Marion street was converted into a
veritable conservatory. Palms and
ferns formed a background of verdant
green, for the enmassment of spring's
rarest and most gorgeous blossoms.

Promptly at 6 o'clock the two young
people took their places before the im-
provised floral altar, where Dr. Wil-
liam Greenburg of Temple Emmanuel
pronounced the impressive ceremony
that made them man and wife.

After congratulations had been offered, the guests partook of a wedding supper, at a handsomely laid table, decorated in pink and white. A
number of out-of-town relatives were
in attendance.

The bride, who is of the Gibson type
of beauty, looked charming in an exquisite traveling costume of blue rajah
cloth, made with a pinafore jacket and
plaited skirt, and waist of eyelet em-
broidery, trimmed in real Valenciennes
lace.

Mr. and Mrs. Neiman are now at
home at the Hotel Worth in this city.

relying on the tried and true, Carrie courageously bought the newest and most sophisticated styles, paying special attention to fine fabrics, clean lines and superb workmanship. She saw her salary more than double, to $25 a week, making her one of the highest paid women in Dallas. She was already a stand-out, and she was only getting started.

Page 34. Al Neiman photographed in Fort Worth, Texas with Herbert Marcus standing on porch. 1910.

Page 38-39. A postcard of Hillsboro, Texas.

Page 42. Mr. and Mrs. A.L. Neiman wedding announcement in the Fort Worth Telegram, April 1905.

CHAPTER THREE

Homesick in Atlanta

L eon Harris, a former vice president at A. Harris and grandson of the store's founder, says in his book *Merchant Princes* that Carrie (whom he describes as Herbert's "slim, dark, doe-eyed, pre-Raphaelite younger sister") became one of the store's best saleswomen, despite not having an extensive formal education and never having traveled far, except in her mind and in the world of books and articles: "She revealed a sure sense of fashion not only extraordinary for an uneducated and untraveled woman not yet twenty, but one never equaled either by her brother or her nephew Stanley and not surpassed by any other American retailer."

In addition to her exemplary retail skills and eye for quality goods, Carrie was stunningly beautiful, and she caught the eye of several Texas gentlemen inside and outside the store. Among her many admirers was Abraham Lincoln Neiman, called Al because of his initials. He was taken with Carrie the moment he met her. "Carrie had a regal bearing," *D* magazine writer Tom Peeler observed in 1984, "a striking composure and an enchanting gaze that could make a gentleman swoon. Al undertook a whirlwind courtship of this pearl of the Texas prairie."

Al Neiman was born on the Fourth of July 1880 in Pittsburgh and grew up in Ohio, in the Cleveland Jewish Orphans Home. Not much is known about his early years, other than that life in the orphanage, not surprisingly, was miserable. With only a grade-school education, he left Cleveland as a teenager to become a traveling salesman, or, as it was known in those days, a "drummer." By the time he was 24, Al was living in Fort Worth and had started a profitable business called American Salvage Company.

His job was putting on sales. That consisted of helping merchants sell their markdowns (and even augmenting the sale merchandise by skillfully buying closeouts from manufacturers) by whatever flamboyant means could be assembled: a brass band or drum-and-bugle corps, a fire department parade, hyperbolic banners promising unbelievable bargains hanging across the town's main street. In the days before movies, radio or television, Al's street theater was free entertainment. It brought out most of a town's citizens and attracted farm families from miles around. "Al had an amazing ability to whip up excitement and help less

Page 44. Carrie Neiman's passport photo, 1905.

Page 47. Al Neiman's passport photo, 1905.

imaginative merchants get rid of their mistakes," according to Leon Harris.

Although it was mostly small country-store merchants who hired Al to sell their markdowns, occasionally finer stores in larger cities hired him, including A. Harris. Although it's a bit unclear how Al Neiman met Carrie Marcus, it is likely that they were introduced in January 1905, when Al was putting on a sale for A. Harris. When they talked for the first time, Carrie was swept off her feet by the handsome and engaging, though sometimes self-centered, Al.

After a short courtship, they were married by a justice of the peace, on April 25, 1905. Carrie was 21; Al was 25. Physically, they were a good match — both tall, slim, dark and handsome. But not everyone thought it was a match made in heaven. Carrie's nephew Stanley Marcus wrote in his 1974 book *Minding the Store* that Carrie was "the essence of kindness and gentleness, with a reserved manner[,] which caused many of her friends to wonder how she could have been attracted to the flamboyant and egotistical Al Neiman."

Like his brother-in-law Herbert — a big dreamer who worked hard in the retail business — Al had big plans for American Salvage Company. He was ready to make his own starry ambitions a reality, and he told whoever would listen. Shortly after he and Carrie married, he convinced his wife and brother-in-law to partner with him in the salvage business and move to Atlanta, Georgia, which Al believed was a wealthier and more sophisticated city than Dallas.

After Atlanta was rebuilt in the wake of the Civil War, it had begun to grow, not only as part of the antebellum cotton-plantation economy but as a distribution and manufacturing center. Al, ever the salesman, convinced Carrie and Herbert that his company would be an even greater success in Atlanta than it had been in Texas. Herbert was immediately open to the idea, largely because of a recent stumble on his own career path: He was working at Sanger Brothers, when in 1905 his new young wife became pregnant with their first child. With his family expanding, Herbert went to the store's president, Alex Sanger, and asked for a raise. Sanger offered Herbert a meager $1.87 a week raise. According to Leon Harris, "The offer was not only insufficient for his growing need but, perhaps more important, it so wounded the growing ego of the poverty-proud Marcus that he quit." Decades later, when Marcus's own store became far grander and more famous than Sanger Brothers, Herbert liked to say that if Alex Sanger had only offered him a bigger raise, he probably would have remained at Sanger Brothers and never built Neiman Marcus as competition.

Atlanta, at the turn of that century, was no larger than Dallas, and to Carrie and Herbert it did not seem more sophisticated, despite what Al had promised. But with Herbert, Carrie and Al all working at putting on sales, the company's profits soared. Merchants in rural areas outside of Atlanta were drawn to the spectacle that the company provided and the instant relief when they were able to get rid of unwanted merchandise or simply raise cash for their stores. The threesome provided their clients excellent customer service, and Al especially was riding high on his financial success. Within only months of their arrival in Atlanta, however, not all was well in the family, which now included Herbert's wife, Minnie, and their 1-year-old son, Stanley. Despite their sizable income, Carrie and Herbert were as unhappy as Al was happy.

Unlike the orphaned Al, Carrie and Herbert had a cultured upbringing. As children they had enjoyed classical music, literature in several languages and intellectual discussion at home. And they never had the appearance of being people of little means. "Aunt Carrie was an extraordinary woman," Stanley Marcus wrote. "She possessed a queenly quality which she carried as if to the manner born. She and my father were born with an appreciation for beauty and fine quality. They were both perfectionists early in their lives, and concurred with Oscar Wilde's declaration, 'I have the simplest tastes. I am easily satisfied with the best.'"

Carrie and Herbert were sophisticated and had refined tastes, but the business they were in was anything but refined. They finally admitted to Al that they viewed the salvage business as an unsavory way to make a living. They explained that they longed to open an exclusive women's ready-to-wear store in Dallas and to have a lifestyle not unlike those of the Sanger and Harris families, for whom they had worked. Herbert and Carrie spent their evenings talking about fine quality garments and the kind of elegant, cultured way of life they hoped to enjoy one day.

There was one other reason that Carrie and Herbert wanted to return to Texas. Both were terribly homesick for their larger family, to whom they were deeply devoted. Al did not have family, other than his new wife, Carrie, and clearly did not feel the same desperate longing to return to Dallas. But, bowing to his wife's and brother-in-law's strong wish, he agreed to do so.

Harold Stanley Marcus
, his Daddy.

Page 48. *The young married couple, Al and Carrie Neiman, 1905.*

Page 53. *"Harold Stanley Marcus and his Daddy." Stanley Marcus photographed with his father, Herbert Marcus, in Atlanta, Georgia, 1906.*

"I Marvel at My Courage on that First Buying Trip"

L eaving Atlanta after less than two years was not as hasty or irrational as it might have appeared to an outsider. The partners already had two attractive buyout offers for their company. One of the offers was from an Atlanta merchant for $25,000 in cash. The other offer came from a firm trying to sell the Missouri or Kansas franchise of a product founded twelve years earlier called Coca-Cola. The threesome, all still in their 20s, decided that operating a Coca-Cola franchise would be too risky. They were not going to be duped by a sugary soft drink that sold at soda fountains for five cents a glass and that, while popular at the moment, might not have staying

power. Instead, they chose what they considered the safer
bet — $25,000 cash.

Decades later, Stanley Marcus liked to tell friends and as-
sociates that Neiman Marcus was founded on a poor business
decision: his father's, aunt's and uncle's choice to take cash for
their company rather than a franchise in what would become
one of the most successful and popular products in American
history. If in the long run it was a poor choice, in the short
term it offered just what they were searching for, the cash to
pursue their dream of opening an exclusive women's ready-
to-wear store in Dallas.

They already had the right stuff to run such an enterprise. They had experience in buying, selling and promotion,
and they recognized fine quality. Physically, all three of them,
tall and imposing, made a great first impression. Still, most
people would have considered their proposition to be daunt-
ing at the least. As Stanley Marcus wrote in *Minding the Store*,
"It took courage to come into the same town dominated by
Sanger Brothers. But courage they didn't lack, nor were they
bashful or overly modest in their evaluation of their own standards of good taste and fashion."

To Dallas's already successful merchants, what Carrie,
Al and Herbert were planning to do seemed "risky to the
point of foolhardiness," writes Leon Harris in *Merchant
Princes*. "They proposed to open a frankly expensive store
(years before the oil boom) in a town as yet far from rich.
Even riskier was their insistence that this store's high-priced

clothing would not be custom-made but ready-to-wear."
Harris continues:

> Fashionable rich women of Dallas in 1907 still had
> their clothes made to order in New York, and by the
> best local dressmakers, including Miss Ward of Sanger
> Brothers, Madame Bartel of A. Harris & Co., and
> Titche-Goettinger's Madame Snow. Neiman Marcus
> promised that its revolutionary ready-made clothes
> would be even finer than made-to-order fashions. To
> ensure the proper fit for these off-the-rack outfits,
> Neiman Marcus hired Madame Bartel away from A.
> Harris & Co., but made plain that she would only fit
> and alter ready-made fashions — thus offering the
> best of both worlds.
>
> The 'piece-goods' department of most fashion
> stores of that era was usually the most important con-
> tributor to the store's reputation, turnover and profits.
> The department supplied both the store's dressmak-
> er and the many private dressmakers then in every
> community, as well as the great majority of women
> who made their own clothes and their family's clothes.
> Neiman Marcus had no piece-goods department.

Carrie, Al and Herbert, now with $25,000 in hand,
pooled their savings and sought financial help from family
members. Carrie's and Herbert's oldest brother, Theo, had

become a successful cotton broker and contributed to the startup business. He and other family members were given minority shares in the new enterprise in exchange for their contributions. In the end, the threesome would have approximately $50,000 to open a store. In early 1907 — with an opening day estimated for August or September — they began to work on their new endeavor, carefully dividing up responsibilities. Herbert would be in charge of the books and would write most of the store's advertisements, while Al was in charge of promotion. Together Herbert and Al handled the finances and logistics of securing a space in a downtown Dallas building.

Carrie had only one job, but it was the most critical job of all. She was in charge of buying all of the merchandise for the new store. Carrie traveled by train to New York on an initial buying trip, armed with only her own fashion sense and a vague idea of what types of materials and styles her future clientele might want. She stayed close to her original ideas of fashion — sophisticated, clean lines and good-quality materials — and returned with some of the latest women's styles from New York and Paris to present to her husband and brother. In an interview years later with the *Christian Science Monitor*, Carrie recalled, "I marvel at my courage on that first buying trip." She knew that the store's hopes for success were completely dependent on her choosing the right clothes, clothes that her brand-new thus far unknown customers would want. Should she choose the wrong garments, the store would fail before it even got started.

In total, she purchased $17,000 worth of merchandise, the very best clothing in satin, silk, taffeta and wool. The merchandise was the new enterprise's largest expense. Furnishing the store with light fixtures, carpet and display cases cost $12,000. Rent was another $9,000. Carrie need not have worried about her buying abilities: Within a month of Neiman Marcus's opening, the entire stock of merchandise had sold out.

They chose for their location a fifty-foot storefront in a four-story building in the heart of the retail district, at the corner of Elm and Murphy streets. Dallas had grown to a city of 86,000 by 1907, nearly doubling in size in the time that Carrie, Al and Herbert were in Atlanta. Now Dallas seemed, in the threesome's eyes at least, primed for a beautiful retail store. But just as they were set to open Neiman Marcus, both Carrie and Herbert became seriously ill. Herbert came down with typhoid fever and couldn't leave his bed. Carrie had suffered a miscarriage a few weeks earlier and was still in critical condition in Millikin Hospital on Akard Street downtown. As a result, on Neiman Marcus's opening day, the only store principal on hand to greet shoppers was Al. The egotistical Al probably enjoyed having all of the focus on himself, although he did have help with customer requests from a staff of thirty-five salespeople.

What was remarkable to many citizens of Dallas was the youth of the owners of the exciting new enterprise. Herbert was barely 29, Al 27 and Carrie only 24. But the language that they used in their first advertising of Neiman Marcus

made clear that although they were young, they were not novices. They had impeccable taste and great confidence in themselves and their judgment, and they understood promotion as well as any merchants in the Southwest.

On Sunday, September 8, 1907, a full-page advertisement appeared in *The Dallas Morning News* announcing "the opening of the New and Exclusive Shopping Place for Fashionable Women, devoted to the selling of Ready-to-Wear Apparel" and naming Neiman Marcus "The Outer-Garment Shop." It stated that "Tuesday, September tenth, marks the advent of a new shopping place in Dallas — a store of Quality, a Specialty store — the only store in the City whose stocks are strictly confined to Ladies' Outer Garments and Millinery and presenting wider varieties and more exclusive lines than any other store in the South." The ad continued:

> Our decision to conduct a store in Dallas was not reached on impulse. We studied the field thoroughly and saw that there was a real necessity for a shopping place such as ours. Our preparations have not been hasty. We have spent months in planning the interior, which is without equal in the South.
>
> *We Will Improve Ready-to-Wear Merchandising.* A store can be bettered by specialized attention. Knowledge applied to one thing insures best results. We began our intended innovation at the very foundation; that is to say with the builders of Women's Garments.

We have secured exclusive lines which have never been shown in Texas before, garments that stand in a class alone as to character and fit.

Our Styles. All the pages of all the fashion journals, American and Foreign, can suggest no more than the open book of realism now here, composed of Suits, Dresses and Wraps of every favored style. The selection will meet every taste, every occasion and every price.

Our Qualities and Values. As well as the Store of Fashions we will be known as the Store of Quality and Superior Values. We shall be hypercritical in our selections. Only the finest productions of the best garment makers are good enough for us. Every article of apparel shown will bear evidence, in its touches of exclusiveness, in its chic and grace and splendid finish, to the most skillful and thorough workmanship.

Another newspaper advertisement for the Store described the principals this way:

Mr. A. L. Neiman is a businessman of conceded ability and as a thorough judge of merchandise has few equals. Mr. Herbert Marcus has for several years been at the head of a department in one of the leading establishments of Dallas, and is well and

favorably known to the shoppers in Dallas. Mrs. A. L. Neiman, formerly Miss Carrie Marcus, who is at the head of the buying and general floor manager for the new firm, is too well known to Dallas shoppers to need an introduction. Mrs. Neiman's judgment in the matter of correct and artistic dress has long been recognized as authority by the most exacting buyers of women's garments.

Page 54. A portrait of Carrie Neiman, ca. 1907. Photograph by Deane Granville.

Page 58-59. Streetcars on Elm Street in downtown Dallas, Texas, in the 1920s.

Page 62-63. First Neiman Marcus store, front right corner, photographed on Elm Street facing Murphy, ca. 1907.

Page 66. Carrie Marcus's bridal portrait, April 1905.

A Way of Doing Business That Would Last for Years

T heir advertising did a great job of convincing readers that only the finest quality items would be available at the Store. In fact, it did too great a job. Potential customers were left with the impression that all that top-quality merchandise would translate to sky-high prices. Within days, Al was forced to put out another advertisement, which amounted to a correction, stating clearly that, although the Store did offer the highest quality merchandise, it was, nevertheless, affordable. He explained that the women's garments being offered were available at several price points.

Many of the wide-eyed visitors to the Store on opening day were there just to see and not to buy, but many shared their opinions about the new Store. One visitor's impressions were recorded in the pages of *Fortune* magazine. That visitor, who was from New York, exclaimed, "I saw dresses that tied those in L. P. Hollander's on Fifth Avenue. Absolutely stunning evening gowns. Coats tailored to beat the band. Furs that must have come from Revillon Freres."

Despite the hard work and planning by the owners, the timing of the Store's opening was hardly propitious. In October, just a month after the Store opened, the nation's economy was badly shaken by the money panic of 1907. A financial crisis was set off by a frenzy of bank withdrawals caused by public distrust of the nation's banking system, and almost overnight the panic wiped out thirteen New York banks and bankrupted several major railroads. People from coast to coast stopped spending. The nation's economy ground to a halt. The panic, which would drag on for months, was so devastating that it led to the creation of the nation's Federal Reserve System.

Still, as if operating in an economic vacuum, Neiman Marcus enjoyed opening months of great success. As customers poured into the Store, the new buyer, Miss Cullen, as she was called — a young woman in her early 20s who had worked at R. H. Sterne in Boston — had to return to New York to replenish the stock. Moira Cullen had a quick and discerning eye for quality and good designs that would appeal to Texas customers. Although the buying budget was quite small, with her excellent sense of style and determination and aggressiveness, she and Carrie were able to fill the stockroom.

Elm and Murphy Streets, Dallas

"The Outer-Garment Shop"

Cordially Invite You to Attend the Formal Opening of the New and Exclusive Shopping Place for Fashionable Women, Devoted to the Selling of Ready-to-Wear Apparel

Opening Day, Tuesday, September Tenth, from 10 A. M. to 10 P. M.   A Fashion Show Pre-eminent—Artistic Souvenirs

Tuesday, September Tenth, marks the advent of a new shopping place in Dallas—a store of Quality, a Specialty store—the only store in the City whose stocks are strictly confined to Ladies' Outer-Garments and Millinery, and presenting wider varieties and more exclusive styles in these lines than any other store in the South.

All are cordially invited to attend the Opening, to view the initial presentment of the most advanced and authoritative styles in Ready-to-Wear Apparel for Fall and Winter, to accept one of the handsome Souvenirs which will be distributed in honor of the occasion.

Our Store

In extending you an invitation to be present at the opening of the new store on Tuesday, September Tenth, we present herewith some of our claims to your valuable patronage.

Our decision to conduct a store in Dallas was not reached on impulse. We studied the field thoroughly and saw that there was a real necessity for such a shopping place as ours.

Our preparations have not been hasty. We have spent months in planning the interior, which is without an equal in the South.

We Will Improve Ready-to-Wear Merchandising

A store can be bettered by specialized attention.

Knowledge applied to one thing insures best results.

We began our intended innovation at the very foundation; that is to say, with the builders of Women's Garments.

We have secured exclusive lines which have never been shown in Texas before, garments that stand in a class alone as to character and fit.

Buying Facilities

Backed by the best sort of buying connections in every market, stocked by a corps of skilled buyers, managed by an experienced and expert store management, we are confident of our value-giving supremacy, and no store in the country where qualities and styles equal to ours are sold can offer lower prices.

Our Styles

All the pages of all the fashion journals, American and Foreign, can suggest no more than the open book of realism now here, composed of Suits, Dresses and Wraps of every favored style.

For the most important occasion of Formal Dress.

For the Informal afternoon call.

For Shopping or Business wear.

The selection will meet every taste, every occasion and every price.

Our Qualities and Values

As well as the Store of Fashions we will be known as the Store of Quality and Superior Values.

We shall be hypercritical in our selections. Only the finest productions of the best garment makers are good enough for us. Every article of apparel shown will bear evidence, in its touches of exclusiveness, in its chic and grace and splendid finish, to the cleverest designing and the most skillful and thorough workmanship.

Opening Souvenirs

As a memento of the occasion we will present a handsome Souvenir to visitors on opening day. These Souvenirs will be worthy of the offerings of the new store.

Carrie had recovered from her miscarriage and came to the Store within a week after the opening, but it was three months before Herbert felt well enough to work.

The new Store shocked and impressed anyone who had doubted whether unsophisticated Dallas would support such a high-end place like Neiman Marcus. Years later Carrie would remember the early planning and how many people had asked her why high style and ready-made clothes were necessary in a city whose streets were unpaved — and when wealthy ladies still had their clothes made by personal seamstresses. In other words, *Why should a store so far from New York or Paris have ready-made clothes? Who would buy European-inspired clothes?*

In her elegant and patrician way, Carrie simply insisted that the Neiman Marcus specialty store would not only meet the needs of the growing middle-class and upper-class women of the city but also contribute greatly to the "growth, welfare and culture of Dallas."

She was, of course, right. And instead of turning off customers, the fact that the clothes were ready-to-wear appealed greatly to the earliest clientele. In advertising director Zula McCauley's fifty-year history of Neiman Marcus, she wrote, "'You save us the bother of having our clothes made,' said some customers. 'You save us the long trip to New York or Paris to shop; now we can go there and enjoy ourselves,' said others."

While working as the main buyer for the Store in the early years, Carrie continued to develop her fashion sense and build a reputation for elegant, wearable couture. She always insisted that there were "no rules" in the fashion business, apart from following one's own taste and style with modest guidance from larger trends. Carrie made an art form of studying colors and fabrics from European catalogues and magazines, then applying them to her vision of clean, simple and feminine design. For decades she would direct others in the Store to purchase only high-quality materials and to give them a "Neiman Marcus style," for example, by replacing "garish buttons, pins and belt buckles with simpler ornamentation."

Herbert Marcus, too, was equally fanatical about that quality and staying true to the "Neiman Marcus style." Well after World War II, every piece of ready-to-wear clothing was put on a form and thoroughly inspected. If any detail of fit, any handmade buttonhole, the pressing and shaping of a suit lapel, or the hang of a skirt was less than the best, the garment was returned to the manufacturer. It was an expensive way to run a business, but it paid off with the loyalty of eager and appreciative customers, many of whom began to come from all over Texas and the South.

Shoppers, whose skirts swept the floor in the Store's earliest days and whose waistlines were hourglass small, knew that they might pay more for a suit and hat at Neiman Marcus, but they also knew that the quality of the item justified the price. The cuts, the looks and the fabrics were all the finest and freshest and were meant to last. In the heart of Texas, customers were enjoying the same haute couture quality experienced by shoppers in New York, San Francisco, London and

Page 68. A portrait of Minnie Lichtenstein Marcus with her sons (left to right), Edward, Stanley, Herbert, and Lawrence, ca. 1919.

Page 71. First Neiman Marcus advertisement announcing the opening of the store, written by Herbert Marcus for the Dallas Morning News, *September 5, 1907.*

Page 72. A portrait of Herbert Marcus, 1921.

Page 73. A portrait of Carrie's father, Jacob Marcus, 1921.

Page 76. A painting of Carrie Neiman, artist unknown.

Rome. Giving the women of Dallas the finest fabrics from the start was a winning strategy. Other merchants in Texas simply watched in awe as Neiman Marcus exceeded all expectations — and turned a profit even in the Store's earliest years.

More than a few outside observers traced the early success to a simple reality: the innumerable hours that Carrie, Herbert and Al spent on the selling floor and in the fitting rooms, working directly with customers. In their regal but somehow unpretentious way, the Store's owners explained exactly what made their clothes more expensive than others and promised that the clothes would differentiate their customers from less demanding peers — just as they differentiated Neiman Marcus from stores less committed to offering the best-made clothing possible.

It was a culture, a way of doing business, that would last for years: With one of the principals on the selling floor guiding a customer as she made her selections, the customer felt special, cared for, cosseted. Dallas had never seen customer service on this level before, but from the very start, the high level of personal service worked like magic.

Even in her later years, when Carrie might be busy placing an important merchandise order or perusing a garment catalogue, searching for the finest materials, she would drop everything to wait on a loyal customer. Stanley Marcus would later explain that although that was inconvenient and time consuming, it was the only way to do it — and it was "the way the business had been built."

CHAPTER SIX

Rebuilding a New Successful Station in Life

In May 1913, a devastating fire destroyed the Store, just five years after it had opened. The family was deeply distraught, feeling that the years of hard work had vanished in the embers and ash. Carrie's brother Theo (she and Herbert often turned to him for advice) told them to sell the Store and salvage whatever they could. But Carrie, Al and Herbert, ever the self-confident optimists, had a different idea entirely. Not only would they reopen, they would do it in a new building with much more space and many more departments. The competing merchants in Dallas frowned and were again convinced that the young threesome were going to over-extend themselves, this time with a new, larger Store. *Surely,*

MARCUS C. EXCLUSIVE WOMEN'S CLOTHIERS

Rogers-
Photo.
DALLAS.

they will face financial ruin, went the thinking. But just like before, the others in town were wrong.

In August 1914, only fifteen months after the fire, the Store opened in a 40,000-square-foot space in a four-story red-brick building at the corner of Main and Ervay streets. Overnight, Neiman Marcus had rocketed from being a small "outer-garment shop" to becoming a "specialty shop." This time there were accessories; lingerie and corsets; clothes for infants, girls and boys; and even a moderately priced Misses Shop.

Carrie was thrilled but still not sitting still. She had continued to devour newspapers and magazines, always trying to improve her knowledge about everything that had to do with fashion, style and taste, just as she had as a child. Like Carrie, Herbert had also become an autodidact, educating himself by setting out to read the *Encyclopedia Britannica* from start to finish. Arthur Kramer, who married into the A. Harris retail store family, tried to put Herbert down by telling people that Herbert was embarrassed by his lack of formal education. Kramer liked to joke that "when you heard him expound on Dickens or Dostoevsky, you knew he was in Volume D. But he became successful so fast that he gave it up in the middle of Volume M, and, therefore, if you ask him about Thackery and Tolstoy, he thinks it's a cloak and suit manufacturer on Seventh Avenue."

In *Merchant Princes*, Leon Harris wrote: "Kramer, of course, meant the anecdote to diminish Marcus, but on

Neiman-Marcus Company

Individual Shops for Gentlewomen

DALLAS

Page 78. Herbert Marcus and sons (from top) Stanley, Edward, Herbert Jr. and Lawrence.

Page 80-81. The first Neiman-Marcus store on Elm and Murphy after the fire in 1913.

Page 83. An early advertisement for Neiman-Marcus, ca. 1927.

most people who knew both men it had the opposite effect. It illustrated the peevish envy Kramer felt for Marcus's obviously far greater abilities, an envy that led Kramer to imitate Marcus in business. And it illustrated Marcus's irresistible determination to achieve by hard work in every area of his life those things that were most important to him."

When Carrie and Al had first returned to Dallas from Atlanta, they moved into the home of Carrie's sister Minnie and her husband, Abe Rosenbaum. Carrie adored her older sister and loved spending time with her. But in 1923, she and Al moved into their imposing three-story home on a large corner lot on Swiss Avenue. The 5,100-square-foot house had a grand staircase just past the front door, as well as an elevator. The sweeping living and dining rooms were perfect for entertaining. Elegantly and tastefully appointed, it was the kind of expansive, formal edifice that fit the Neimans' new successful station in life.

It is the house where I would come to meet my great aunt Carrie — without, at first, understanding the amazing legendary arc of her life.

Page 85. Carrie Neiman's foyer in her Swiss Avenue home in Dallas, Texas.

Always the Elegant Lady

A
l Neiman had never been known as reserved, but his ostentatious and flamboyant ways seemed to multiply with the growing success of the Store.

With more money and status to his name, Al was determined to make up for his miserable childhood as an orphan. He used his enormous energy to live life to the fullest — which, to him, meant having as much fun as possible. He loved good food and drink, gambling and, most especially, women. In the early days of Dallas, affairs by married men of a certain income were not only acceptable but practically de rigueur, provided they were discreet. But Al was anything but discreet. He fancied and openly flirted with practically every

attractive woman who passed him on the street, and that was
shocking enough. But a number of his flagrant affairs were
with saleswomen in the Store — the Store that his wife helped
build and run, and where she spent most of her waking hours.
Al's constant extramarital affairs were obvious and painful
to the hardworking and stoic Carrie, but for years she simply
turned her head as if to ignore the adulteries.

Al was breaking Carrie's heart, and by the mid 1920s
he also was making life miserable for Herbert. Al had become
contrary and difficult, stymieing one important business
decision after another. In Herbert's mind, beyond being egotistical, Al was opinionated and argumentative but most of
all volatile — and not just when he was alone in an office
with Herbert. One minute Al would be out on the selling floor,
smiling and complimenting a saleswoman for the job she was
doing, and the next minute he would be yelling at her in front
of other workers and even customers.

Al, feeling set upon, asked Carrie whether her loyalties
were with the Marcus family or with him. He insisted that
Carrie often sided with Herbert rather than with him during
family or business disagreements. He said it bothered him to
no end. Adding to the conflict and tension at the Store was
the return in 1926 of Herbert's eldest son, Stanley, home from
Harvard and, as the first family member with a college degree,
anxious to offer his many opinions about retailing.

The bickering continued for months until Herbert, Carrie
and Al agreed that the battles were bad for business. The only

solution was to part ways. They agreed on a price for the Store of $250,000 and that Herbert would buy out Al's interest with funds from a bank. Carrie had tried to remain neutral in the dissolution agreement, but soon after the buyout, she had her own deeply personal issues with Al. After years of reticence with regard to his many dalliances, she decided to confront her husband about rumors that he was having an affair with one of the Store's buyers. It was hardly the first time that such a rumor had circulated. But this time, Al admitted it was true. Carrie finally had had enough. In 1928, at the age of 45, she sued Al for divorce.

The case was heard in Judge Webster Atwell's court just blocks from the Store, and it did not begin well for Al: "Young man," Judge Atwell pronounced, "you have come into my court with dirty hands." In 1920s America, an enormous stigma was connected with divorce. In some cases, just the label "divorced" could ruin a woman's reputation for life. But while longtime customers and friends of the Neimans initially took sides in the company dissolution and the divorce, most people eventually came to side with Carrie. The fun-loving, high-flying Al had his admirers, but friends and customers also could see that Al was at times intolerable and that he treated Carrie badly. They still viewed Carrie as the elegant lady — and the victim — that she was.

Divorced or not, Carrie continued to have an extraordinarily good reputation. Although she was heartbroken over the breakup of her marriage, she remained Dallas's chief arbiter of taste and style, and she seemed to suffer very little public stigma. In later years, many customers who saw Carrie working at the Store from dawn until dusk, and who had never known or heard of Al, assumed that she was never married and, in the parlance of the day, an old maid.

One of the conditions of the business dissolution was that Al, then 48, would not work in retail in Dallas for ten years. In his typically arrogant way, Al ignored the agreement and only months later brashly joined Woolf Brothers of Kansas City, which owned Dreyfus and Company in Dallas, located directly across the street from Neiman Marcus. Believing Al had violated their noncompete contract, Herbert successfully sued Al in federal court to remove him from Woolf Brothers.

Years later, Al would try to reconnect with Carrie, presumably to rekindle their marriage. Carrie's sister Minnie learned about Al's plans and pleaded with Carrie not to take him back. Whether or not she was influenced by Minnie, Carrie had only minimal contact with her ex-husband, and she rarely spoke his name again.

Al eventually moved to Kansas City, then Chicago and finally New York, where he opened a firm called Goldring Neiman that handled women's departments for several big-city stores, but it was not a large success. In the 1950s, he started his own New York purchasing firm, but it soon failed. Although he would make several attempts at new businesses, he would never be involved with a company remotely as successful as Neiman Marcus. In his later years, Al moved back to Texas and lived with very few possessions (he claimed he had only one

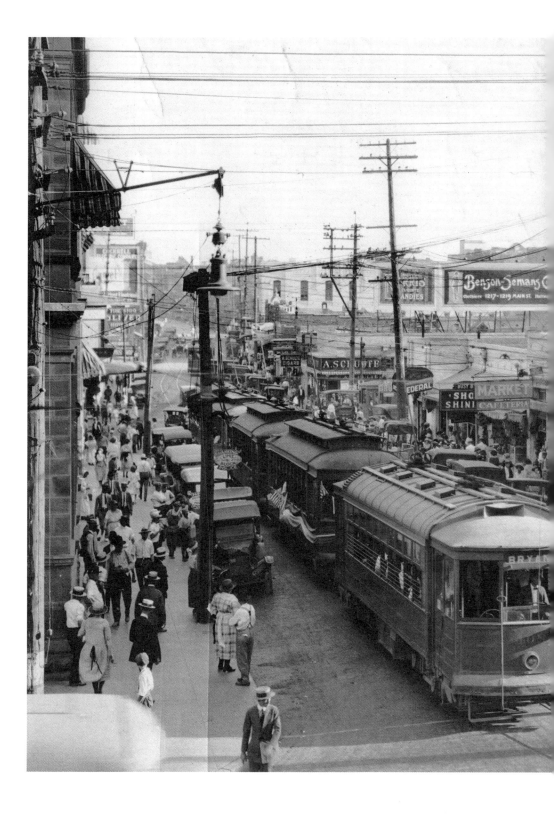

gold cufflink to his name) and very little money at the Masonic Temple in Arlington. By his 80s Al was penniless and alone, but he did try one last time to make some money with a book about the Store. He talked about it with a *Dallas Morning News* writer, who interviewed him several times before concluding that Al's memory was unreliable and a book would be impossible.

Al died in the Home for Aged Masons in Arlington at the age of 95, on October 21, 1970.

Page 86. Al and Carrie Neiman photographed in an unknown location.

Page 89. Portrait of Stanley Marcus. 1932. Photographer unknown.

Page 92-93. Neiman-Marcus building (on right) on Ervay looking south from Main, Dallas, ca. 1920.

Page 95. A script for television news announcing Al Neiman's death. 1970.

ABE MARCUS NEIMAN

      The co-founder of the Neiman-Marcus Company,

Abrahaim Lincoln Neiman, died yesterday in Arlington.

He was 95.

      With Herbert Marcus, Neiman established the

widely known specialty store in Dallas in 1907.

      He left Dallas in 1928 to be become active in

a number of mercantile enterprises in Chicago,

Minneapolis and New York. He also traveled

extensively on buying trips for the Dallas store.

      Neiman returned to Texas about three years ago

to live at the Masonic Home For Aged Masons.

      Funeral services will be held there tomorrow.

The Tall Girl from Dallas

T he larger Marcus family had almost no contact with Al after the divorce, although in 1953, when Al read in *The New York Times* that Carrie had died, he wrote a letter to Stanley. "Just don't know how to start this letter," Al began. He continued:

> To say I was terribly sorry to hear the sad news is expressing my feelings mildly. She was a proud and noble woman and I am much afraid I caused her much unhappiness. The past is gone and unfortunately can never be recalled. She was a great inspiration to all who knew her. Her foresight and tremendous ability

did much toward making NM the great institution it now is. Deep down in my heart believe me I say a prayer for her. She has gone to heaven and may God rest her soul. My deepest sympathy to all the family.

Sincerely, Al Neiman

Al clearly had seen the error of his ways, but perhaps far too late.

Some years after Al and Carrie divorced, according to Frank X. Tolbert in his book *Neiman Marcus Texas*, Carrie and Al were seated one row apart at a New York theater. "They never corresponded," Tolbert writes, "yet she still shines in his memory."

Tolbert quotes Al Neiman: "She was a combination of beauty and brains and perfect taste the like of which I don't think this business will ever see again. Frankly, I learned this business from Carrie."

Tolbert adds: "Neiman says that in all the years he lived and worked with Carrie, he never knew her judgment on fashion and merchandising to be wrong. He said that Herbert Marcus the elder leaned heavily on his sister's genius for always doing the right thing. Neiman thinks his ex-wife contributed more than any other person to making Neiman Marcus what it is today."

After the divorce, Carrie continued to live at the large Swiss Avenue home that she had shared with Al. Her sister Minnie and her husband, Abe, continued to live there with her. At the Store, she devoted her attention to the Better Gown Department and to its discriminating customers. She flew to New York to buy fine clothing and ship it back to Dallas for her growing number of dedicated customers.

Legendary tales abound about Carrie's allowing her Texas clients to travel by train with her on buying trips to New York, then outfitting them with wedding trousseaux or young debutante wardrobes. Women continued to rely on her discerning expertise in what was tasteful and fashionable. She would send limousines to Dallas hotels (usually the grand Beaux Arts–inspired Adolphus, built by the founder of the Anheuser-Busch dynasty) to pick up special out-of-town customers who had arrived in the city just to shop at the Store. She was omnipresent, with a soothing and wise aura on the selling floor. No situation was too complex for her to handle. Carrie could even calm a frightened bride, who would gratefully respond by buying a gown and trousseau from her.

After Al left the business, Stanley was given some of his responsibilities, including exerting financial control over the Store's two main clothing buyers — Carrie and Moira Cullen. Stanley wrote in *Minding the Store* that neither Carrie nor Moira "had ever shown much interest in fiscal responsibility. They both loved beautiful things and would never pass a desirable garment, however overbought they might be ... they were buyers with courage, taste, fashion awareness and a non-compromising understanding of quality."

NEIMAN
NEW YORK

March 10 - 1953.

Dear Stanley,-

Just don't know how to
start this letter.

To say I was terribly sorry
to hear the sad news is
expressing my feelings mildly
She was a grand and noble
woman & I am much afraid
I caused her much unhappiness.
The past is gone and unfortunately
can never be recalled.

She was a great inspiration
to all who knew her -
Her foresight and tremendous

1407 BROADWAY   NEW YORK 18. N.Y.   LONGACRE 3-0734

ability did much toward
making NM the great
institution it now is.
Deep down in my heart
believe me I say my prayers
for her.
She has gone to Heaven
and may God rest her Soul.
My deepest sympathy to
all the family —

Sincerely
Al Neiman

1407 BROADWAY   NEW YORK 18, N.Y.   LONGACRE 3-0734

The two buyers were neither afraid nor reticent when it came to telling New York manufacturers exactly what they needed for the Store. "In looking at a line," Stanley wrote:

Aunt Carrie would remark, "That dress has a ray-on binding. We must change it to pure silk, for our customers won't accept rayon." It probably cost the maker $1.50 to make the change, but he acceded without undue argument. They would agonize for thirty minutes over the selection of the quality of lace to go into a ball gown, or the best shade of black for a winter coat purchase. Aunt Carrie and Miss Cullen weren't designers and they had no false illusions about it. But they were creators of a style, a Neiman Marcus style.

Moira Cullen was, in fact, so influential in New York that in 1928 she persuaded fashion houses to create a "step-in" dress that buttoned up the front to avoid the hair-messing that pullover dresses caused. Stanley Marcus would later call this shirt-waisted dress "a major contribution to the dress market." Moira, who never married and lived with her brother, became very close with Carrie. Both women worked hard and were all business during work hours, but when they were on a buying trip in New York or abroad, they enjoyed a night out together.

Through their bond and friendship, Carrie maintained

an uncanny, prescient ability to see the future of fashion. Beginning in the 1920s, no one at the Store — or at any other major specialty store in America — had Carrie's ability to predict upcoming trends. "Carrie's major quality was her ability to smell the future," Harris writes. "She instinctively knew which colors would be 'in' next spring, which cut of dress was not too risque for her clients but would be discreet enough to be enticing."

Still, she was never overbearing. Stanley said of his aunt, "She had strong convictions about what she liked and didn't like, but she was probably the most modest woman I have ever known." Even when she told New York manufacturers exactly what she needed, she did it in an unthreatening way. Manufacturers did not fear her, but they did respect her, and — modest or not — she usually got what she wanted from them.

Author Frank Tolbert says that Al Neiman told him about an early buying trip in which he and Carrie looked at some pleated skirts in the salon of a leading New York City wholesaler. Writes Tolbert:

> The tall girl from Dallas looked over the pleated skirts and she was silent. Finally the wholesaler asked her directly what she thought.
>
> Carrie said, "I'm sorry you asked me that. I just don't like the skirts."
>
> The dealer protested that Lanvin and other Paris

houses were showing nothing else, and that all important New York manufacturers were showing pleats. Carrie was unconvinced.

Tolbert says that Al told him, "Three months later, there wasn't a pleated skirt on display by any of the leading New York manufacturers. Carrie's hunch that a new style trend was in the offing came true."

Page 96. A portrait of Carrie Neiman wearing her trademark strand of pearls, ca. 1925.

Page 100-101. The letter from Al Neiman to Stanley Marcus upon the death of Carrie Neiman, 1953.

Page 105. A private fashion show at the downtown Neiman Marcus. Photograph by John Rogers, ca. 1955.

A Skill
Perfected by Carrie

W hen Stanley Marcus was still new to the Store, he would marvel at the way his aunt did business. Noticing that Carrie would sometimes interrupt her work to take a particularly good customer to the market in New York to make selections at two or three designer showrooms, he asked her, "How can you afford to devote so much time and effort to a single customer when you are buying for thousands of customers?" Carrie, recognizing a chance to teach her nephew something that might not be immediately obvious, replied, "We can't afford not to. If we don't take care of these unusual requests from women who are depending on us, they might drop in to a competitive store in New York, and then we would lose them for good."

Stanley said, "Many of us thought that Aunt Carrie's taste was infallible, but she disagreed, saying, 'No one's judgment is infallible. It's a mistake to base fashion predictions on the past. There are no rules in the fashion business.'"

In the 1930s, despite the Great Depression, Neiman Marcus continued to serve as a cultural and fashion center in Texas, largely as a result of Carrie's and Stanley's approach to fashion merchandising. Rather than viewing the Store strictly as a place for customers only to purchase high-end items, they wanted it to be a fashion gallery, a place where customers could see items — that they couldn't necessarily buy — from New York and Europe. To this end, during the early 1930s, Carrie began to host elegant Fall Fashion Expositions at the Store. Free of charge, they were style shows of the kind that had rarely occurred outside of New York City. Carrie hired models and dressed them in the latest styles, allowing visitors to Neiman Marcus to become part of the fashion industry and experiment with coordinating outfits using merchandise from the Store's latest collections. The Fall Fashion Expositions were immensely popular, with the Store proving too small to accommodate the hundreds of guests waiting to get a glimpse of Carrie's latest selections.

At the same time that the high-couture shows were taking place, Neiman Marcus, not wanting to turn away customers of lesser means, began offering lower-priced items and providing credit on lenient terms. From the Store's inception, one of the great mysteries of Neiman Marcus is how it managed to

Page 106. Stanley Marcus photographed on his honeymoon after his marriage to Billie Cantrell Marcus. White Sulphur Springs, West Virginia, 1932.

Page 109. Stanley Marcus sits at one side of the runway during a fashion show preview at Neiman Marcus. His father, Herbert, sits across from him, 1945. Photographed for LIFE Magazine by Nina Leen.

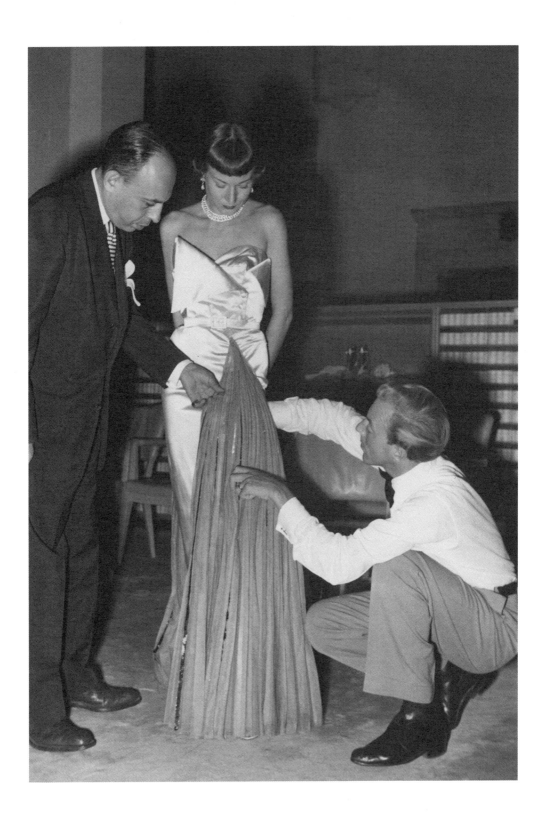

attract the wealthiest customers while at the same time not turning away those with merely average budgets. The question was, *How did the Store go for years offering something at medium price points while maintaining its reputation for giving its clientele only the best?* Stanley Marcus addressed this balancing act when he wrote that to appeal to both price levels "requires a certain skill which does not permit the 'upper crust' customer to feel downgraded, nor the 'middle range' customer to feel patronized." It was a skill perfected by Carrie, years before Stanley arrived at the Store. A 1928 advertisement in *The Dallas Morning News* offered women's coats ranging in price from $68.50 to $495, with the wording, "In this smart fashion store, a woman can be sure of getting the correct things ... the choice, new smart thing at its proper and reasonable price."

With the Great Depression running through the 1930s, many storekeepers in Dallas assumed that Herbert and Carrie would be forced to lower their standards, to buy and sell clothing of lesser quality than they had since the Store's inception. But the siblings made a conscious decision that no matter how severe the Depression became they would never compromise on quality. Many observers believed that the Marcus family would have made considerably more money had they relaxed their standards, as most stores did during the Depression, but the Marcuses refused to do so. "They always put quality over profits," said Leon Harris. "They were always far more interested in having a first-rate store than they were in making money."

*Page 110-111. A fashion show in the Zodiac room at the downtown
Neiman Marcus. Photograph by John Rogers, 1955.*

*Page 112. Stanley Marcus and French dress designer Jacques Fath fit a model
for the Neiman Marcus Fortnight. Photograph by John Rogers, 1949.*

Page 114-115. Stanley Marcus fits models before a fashion show.

*Page 116. Stanley Marcus moderates a fashion show at the downtown
Neiman Marcus. Photograph by John Rogers, 1949.*

By the late 1930s, the Store's haute couture reputation helped it gain national accolades. In November 1937, *Fortune* magazine featured Neiman Marcus in an article titled "Dallas in Wonderland," the first time that *Fortune* had focused on a Texas business. The article's author wrote, "Herbert Marcus and his sister Carrie Neiman, and his three sons in the business, have sublimated and channeled every ounce of their considerable selves into four floors of beautiful merchandise." The author noted, "They live the store, not by lacking outside interests but by transferring them all inside. ... A strong moral sense runs through the whole family, uniting them less in a sense of duty toward one another than in a common sense of duty to the store." Carrie might have argued correctly that family members did, indeed, feel a sense of duty to one another, but the author's point that they had a sense of duty to the Store was also very important — and very true.

Collier's magazine also featured the Store in a major spread, as did *Life* magazine in an article that placed Carrie in the spotlight. The 1939 *Life* story, titled "Texas: A Giant State Stirs Itself," featured Carrie working in the Store in a picture essay that highlighted the economic, political and social development of Dallas.

In 1938, Carrie and Stanley once more elevated the status of Neiman Marcus by establishing the Neiman Marcus Awards for Distinguished Service in the Field of Fashion. The awards honored designers, journalists, celebrities and others who had influenced the fashion scene, and Neiman Marcus

became an even more important name in the fashion world, identifying trendsetters, incorporating their styles into store merchandise and attempting to establish the Store as an arbiter of prestige. Carrie and Stanley chose Europeans as well as Americans for the awards, further broadening their scope. Early recipients included Germaine Monteil, a French-born seamstress who moved to New York and established herself in the design of dresses by using bright patterns; Nettie Rosenstein, an Austrian-born lingerie designer; and Dorothy Wright Liebes, a famous American textile designer.

Distinguished Service Awards were later presented to individuals who addressed other issues in fashion and merchandising, including labor rights and safety. New York banker Max Meyer was honored with an award in 1941 for "his part in creating a better world for the clothing industry and his work in solving the sweat-shop problem." Combined with Carrie's New York and European–infused Fall Fashion Expositions, the awards — often referred to as the Oscars of Fashion — brought the Store even more international acclaim.

Page 118-119. (Left to right) Billie, Stanley, Minnie and Herbert Marcus at Grand Central Station during a buying trip to New York.

Page 121. Exterior of Neiman Marcus in downtown Dallas, Texas. Photographed for LIFE Magazine by Alfred Eisenstadt.

CHAPTER TEN

The Remarkably Tight-Knit Marcus Family

A

s the nation recovered from the Great Depression, the Store continued to grow and the profits came in. When Carrie traveled to London on buying trips, she stayed at the magnificent Hotel Claridge. In New York, she booked herself into the famous Waldorf Astoria. When she spent a month during the summer in New York buying fall lines, she rented a spacious, sprawling home on Long Island. The home had to be large enough to accommodate Carrie's many siblings and their children and grandchildren, as well. After Carrie and Al divorced, Carrie's sister Minnie often accompanied Carrie on her buying trips to New York and Europe.

Minnie had some peculiarities: She always carried a crisp $20 bill in her purse, which she refused to use — and when she died, it was still in her purse. Carrie always paid when the two went out to dinner or the theater, whether in Dallas, New York or abroad. And although Minnie and her husband lived with her, Carrie did most of the work at the big home on Swiss Avenue. When Minnie wouldn't touch the bandages on her husband, Abe, after his burning accident, it fell to Carrie to change them every day.

Carrie not only paid for many of Minnie's trips and household costs, but she also increasingly paid for her nieces' and nephews' large expenses, including secondary-school and college tuitions. Carrie strongly believed in the importance of education, having had almost no formal education herself. Perhaps because of her generosity, she was allowed and even expected to give her stamp of approval on all important personal relationships within the family, from girlfriends and boyfriends to marriages. Carrie was not just a casual observer of her young relatives. She found time to be with her nieces and nephews, dining with them and taking them to the theater, sometimes to the point of causing resentment among their mothers.

Though Carrie got along well with the younger generation, she was no pushover, and her young relatives did not take advantage of her. She had strong opinions about proper behavior, and in some cases her opinion showed her age. Once, when Carrie was planning to host a family dinner, a niece asked if she could invite a man who was a Russian Jew. Carrie forbade the niece from bringing him because he was of Russian and not German descent, as the Marcuses were. At the time, many German Jews looked down on Russian Jews and blamed them for rampant anti-Semitism. Carrie's feelings about Russian Jews, however, did not seem to carry over to Herbert's wife, Minnie Lichtenstein Marcus, whose Jewish family was from Russia and with whom Carrie got along very well.

Although it was perhaps small-minded or backward of Carrie to refuse to entertain a Russian Jew, in many ways she was enormously progressive. She read current literature and enjoyed contemporary theater and music. However, while she was aware of modern trends in art, she did not care for non-representational art but had a strong preference for masters such as Renoir. Her sense of independence extended to her personal finances. She handled all of her own fiscal matters at a time when most women did not have a bank account. Carrie didn't just work at the Store; she was instrumental in its operations and she sat on the board of directors.

Away from work, Carrie was not overtly religious, but she did attend Temple Emanu-El services on Jewish holidays. She also belonged to the Columbian Club, whose members were mostly Jewish. She had neither the time nor the interest in the pastimes of many other upper-class women of her day, such as belonging to a garden club or bridge group. Although she had many friends, the Store and her family always came

first. Even as years passed and the family grew quite large, she helped the Marcuses to remain a remarkably tight-knit group, carrying on a long tradition of Sunday lunch at Carrie's home on Swiss Avenue, where virtually the only topic of discussion was "the Store."

The time-honored practice of family members walking the floor at Neiman Marcus continued well into the second generation, with Stanley or one of his brothers usually being available to assist a customer.

To be waited on by a member of the family was a special treat for customers, and beyond the immediate family, there was always on hand an abundance of cousins, nieces and nephews. For many years, Carrie's father, Jacob — affectionately known around the Store as "Grampa" — sat by the Main Street entrance, nodding to customers and offering children a piece of hard candy. At one point, there were sixty-two members in the family and many of them were employed at the Store. Stanley said that sometimes the relations made an enormous contribution, sometimes not so much. But, for sure, no family member was ever fired.

Page 122. Herbert Marcus kisses his granddaughter Jerrie Marcus, 2, at his home in east Dallas, Texas. 1938.

Page 124-125. Portrait of Herbert Marcus (seated, left) photographed at home with his family. Photograph by Rogers Studio.

Page 128-129. (Left to right) Roberta Miller (Cohen), Rhea Miller (Schultz), Minnie Rosenbaum, Henry Jacobus, Vera Shultz, Hervin Shultz, Herbert Marcus, Minnie Marcus, Ervill Rosenbaum, Carrie Marcus Neiman, Jean Miller Garfield, Ann Folz and Dorothy Jacobus pose on the front steps of Carrie Neiman's home on Swiss Avenue in Dallas, Texas.

Page 131. Carrie's father, Jacob Marcus, on the ground floor of Neiman-Marcus on opening day, September 1907.

"Child, Come with Me. I'll Show You How It Is Done"

Through the decades — and especially since Carrie's death — much has been written about the iconic Neiman Marcus. But Carrie, in part because she was a woman, was often not given credit for the trailblazing, integral role she played in the Store's founding and early success. According to her nephew Lawrence Marcus, Herbert's youngest son, Carrie was the "real brains of the family," and "she had so many jobs, working with the store's budget that was never large enough, selecting merchandise, understanding the problem of selling, accommodating her customers and always stressing to her salespeople the importance of excellence and service."

In the end, it was Carrie Marcus who was in charge of selecting the merchandise, and it was merchandise, after all, that made Neiman Marcus what it was. Without her, Neiman Marcus might have been just another small specialty store selling nice items that made a bit of profit for its owners. But Carrie had an eye that was unequalled and a magical innate ability to select only the best, which is precisely what made Neiman Marcus distinct from any other store in America. And she clearly passed along her abilities to others in the family: Stanley Marcus, too, would have an eye for the best, but much if not most of what he learned was at his aunt's knee.

Even he knew that no one in the family was better than Carrie at finding just the right look for just the right customer. A famous moment featuring Pauline Trigere, the legendary fashion designer, shows how Carrie's mind and sensibility worked to perfection: In 1942, Pauline had just started her own business and was eager to sell her line at Neiman Marcus. On her way back from a trip to Mexico, she stopped in Dallas and was taken on a tour of the Store by Edward Marcus, Herbert and Minnie's second son.

On the second floor, Pauline met Carrie, who, she said, "looked as regal and poised as the Queen of England," dressed in black with those ubiquitous pearls around her neck and three chunky gold bracelets on her wrist. A wealthy customer suddenly appeared, looking for a special garment and wanting Carrie's immediate assistance. As the two were headed to a fitting room, Carrie said to young Pauline, "Child, come

with me. I'll show you how it is done." Pauline sat mesmer-
ized on a small chair in the corner while Carrie, ensconced in
her own highbacked upholstered chair, ordered salesgirls to
the stockroom to find just the right gown. When that was ac-
complished, they were sent back to find just the perfect shoes,
bag and hat, and then the correct lingerie. After two hours the
sales had been made, the customer was beyond satisfied, and
Carrie had never moved from her chair. Sixty years later, Pauline Trigere remembered that day as the time she learned her
biggest lesson: Know your stock, impeccably, and know the
importance of the intimate and trusting relationship between
a clothier and her customer.

Over the years, the legends multiplied. Sam Fagan, who
worked in the Neiman Marcus shoe department for more than
fifty years, recalled that when he first started at the Store, he
was ordered to bring shoes up to a second-floor fitting room
for a customer Carrie was assisting. Knowing that Mrs. Neiman, as he called her, was very demanding, he worked hard
to gather only the best examples to show. The customer liked
everything that Sam brought, but Carrie said, "Mr. Fagan,
those shoes are not the right shoes for that outfit. Please go
get some more." He dutifully followed her directive and went
back to the stockroom in search of the perfect shoe. In time he
found it. Carrie finally proclaimed of a pair, "This is the right
shoe for you!" The customer was pleased and impressed, and
the young shoe salesman learned that when working with Mrs.
Neiman the only way to make a sale was to make it a perfect

one, no matter how many trips it took to the stockroom. It was part of the DNA, part of the culture, part of the growing and enduring history. It all recalled what Carrie's brother Herbert had used as a mantra, that "no sale is a good sale for Neiman Marcus unless it's a good buy for the customer."

Page 132. Carrie Neiman wearing her famous gold bracelets.

Page 136-137. At opening night of the Metropolitan Opera in Dallas, (left to right), Carrie Neiman, Flora Lowey, Minnie Rosenbaum, Ervill Rosenbaum and Minnie and Herbert Marcus.

Page 139. Stanley Marcus and Herbert Marcus at work.

"They're Marvelous!": Shaping Dallas Society

S ometimes, as Carrie's stature in the city grew, people would ask her what made her proudest of Neiman Marcus. She would frequently reply that it was the Store's contribution to the growth of Dallas. She was proud of her city's growth and maturity, and she believed strongly in giving back to her community. And she was also a fierce patriot, who, along with family members, donated money to the war effort. During World War II, she encouraged customers to buy war bonds, and in some cases she made war bonds the price of admission to her Fall Fashion Expositions, announcing in a 1942 advertisement, "help the war effort and see America's greatest premier of fashion." When certain materials, such as nylon, became scarce during World War II, Carrie sought top fashion experts to create new styles and fabrics for the Store that would conserve much-needed supplies for the war effort. (Stanley served on the Apparel Branch of the War Productions Board and worked with Carrie to offer more simplistic styles, as opposed to the pleated skirts and three-piece suits that were popular at the time but put a severe strain on needed war materials.)

Unlike her wayward ex-husband, Al Neiman, who had traded hard work for hard play once the Store became a success, Carrie (and Herbert) seemed to just work harder with each passing year. During store hours, Carrie rarely found the time for lunch and instead quickly ate a sandwich in one of the fitting rooms. She continued to carefully oversee what the saleswomen were doing, spending a good deal of time out on the second floor, which offered some of the Store's finest clothing and accessories and where a large oil portrait of her hung. The high regard in which the family held Carrie was evidenced by the portrait, which was commissioned by the family and painted by the well-known artist Paul Clemens, who was famous in the 1930s and 1940s for his portraits of Hollywood film stars.

Each day that she was in the Store, Carrie hated to see a customer walk out empty-handed. According to Stanley, if she saw someone leaving the Store without a purchase, Carrie might bring her back to a fitting room and "sell her one, two, or even a dozen garments, some of which the customer had previously seen and rejected." Her brother Herbert, even

Page 140. Dallas skyline at night from the Medical Arts Building.
Photograph by Lloyd M. Long, ca. 1939.

Page 143. A painting of Mrs. Carrie Neiman by California artist Paul
Lewis Clemens. ca. 1951.

Page 144-145. The men's department at Neiman Marcus. Photograph by John Rogers.

Page 146. A painting of Herbert Marcus by Douglas Granvil Chandor, ca. 1957.

in his 60s, when he was beginning to have trouble seeing, was trying to keep up with her and still occasionally prowling the floors at the Store, offering to assist customers with their purchases.

In time, customers not only relied on Carrie for fashion advice but, after having come to know her intimately, confided deep secrets, from their greatest personal triumphs to their biggest disappointments. If a longtime customer had a wandering husband, chances are Carrie knew about him. If another customer needed a new outfit for an occasion with a man who was not her husband, chances are Carrie knew about him too. Customers figured that if Carrie could be trusted to tell the truth about how they looked in a particular outfit — never hesitating to kill a sale if the outfit didn't meet her high expectations — then she could guard their solemn secrets. For years, she probably knew more than anyone about the vagaries of high society in Dallas, and she simply became a vast repository of confidences from so many longtime customers. Some came into the Store to see Carrie even when they did not intend to buy anything. Carrie, after listening carefully to their stories, usually sent them on their way with some good advice — and often a purchase.

Carrie's knowledge, in its way, shaped Dallas society well beyond the clothing that the city's most elegant residents brought home from the Store. Because of Carrie, Neiman Marcus itself was considered Dallas's arbiter of fashion and taste, and that included many areas in addition to fashion. When a

Dallas doyenne was preparing to entertain an important guest, she might call Neiman Marcus to ask for pointers. *What would make an elegant dinner? What to serve and how to serve it?* The Store also received inquiries about travel. *Where would Mrs. Neiman suggest they vacation, and when?* The calls became so frequent that Carrie eventually had to ask others at the Store to help field some of the requests for advice.

If she felt inclined, Carrie did not always wait to be asked but rather volunteered her own original ideas about style, taste, entertaining and excursions. In 1949 she read that the Duke and Duchess of Windsor planned to visit the Mexican ranch of two of the Store's big clients, wealthy Dallas oilman Clint Murchison and his wife, Virginia. Carrie telephoned Virginia with just the right suggestions for preparing the Murchisons' ranch house for the royal visit. "It would be nice if you had some linen hand towels with the Duke and Duchess's monogram and their crest," Carrie offered. Virginia was thrilled with the idea, and equally thrilled when the beautiful linens arrived at the ranch only three days later. Upon seeing the towels, the Duchess waved one at Virginia and exclaimed, "They're marvelous!" Several decades later, Virginia was still grateful to Carrie for her stroke of genius — and still shocked that the Duke and Duchess took all twelve linens home with them.

Page 148-149. On set, in the summer of 1948 at 20th Century Fox.
Beverly Hills, California. (Left to right) Mitch Jericho, Martha Anne
Dugas, Florence Bates, Linda Darnell (star), Carrie Neiman, Della Owens
Rice and Lillian Jenkins.

Page 151. Neiman Marcus promotional image of unidentified model with
a Rolls Royce Silver Cloud I.

The First Branch Store: Being Two Places at Once

A s she aged, Carrie remained unafraid of change. She was often the first to be in favor of an idea that helped to modernize or enlarge the Store, even if it deviated from the way things had always been done. She favored adding a fine jewelry department, when Herbert was reluctant. Stanley wrote:

> Aunt Carrie had, from time to time[,] dabbled in precious jewelry for the store, buying on occasion a ruby-studded bracelet or a sapphire domed ring, always selling them to her personal customers. I was impressed by her success, so I suggested that we open a special department for fine jewelry. The climate

seemed right, with a growing affluent public and a minimum of local competition. Aunt Carrie was all for it but my father had a few reservations based on the capital requirements for such an operation and on his knowledge that jewelry was rarely sold at a fixed price. From the beginning of the store, he had been adamant about maintaining prices, assuring his sales staff and customers that "Neiman Marcus is a one-price store," regardless of the size of the purchase or the name and standing of the customer. After deliberation he told me, "If you can assure me that you won't ever deviate from this policy, then go ahead; but remember, you have a whole store's reputation at stake. You can't cut prices in jewelry without endangering your fur, dress and coat business."

Stanley assured his father that he would remain true to the Store's one-price policy — and he did.

There was one time, however, when Carrie was not in favor of a major change. Perhaps no idea was more unacceptable to her — and to Herbert — than Stanley's desire to install escalators in the Store. Carrie and Herbert said escalators were for department stores, not for a beautiful specialty store such as Neiman Marcus. Stanley disagreed, insisting that specialty stores simply had never used escalators because they could not afford them. He argued that escalators could be designed as an aesthetic feature and would add to rather than

Page 152. Carrie Neiman aboard a cruise.

Page 154. Photograph of the interior for the Neiman Marcus department store. Photograph by John Rogers, 1960.

Page 157. Interior of the Neiman Marcus store at Preston Center, Neiman Marcus's first suburban location, 1954.

subtract from the Store's beauty. After months of debate with his father and aunt, Stanley won the argument, but Carrie insisted, "I'll never ride them, nor will any of our good customers." Stanley brought in a designer who created a hanging garden between the escalators, a design so beautiful that it would be widely copied. But true to her word, Carrie never did ride the escalators.

In December 1950, at the age of 72, Herbert Marcus had a severe stroke and died a few days later. The Store's board of directors elected Carrie, then 66, chairman of the board and Stanley president and chief operating officer. As board chairman, Carrie would oversee the opening of Neiman Marcus's first branch store, at Preston Center in suburban North Dallas. She was opposed initially to the expansion and was vocal in her objection, arguing that with two stores the family would lose some of its control over the day-to-day running of the enterprise, control that was essential in maintaining the highest standards. In her particular case, it would be impossible for her to be two places at once, both downtown and in suburban Dallas. But she ultimately acceded to Stanley's insistence that expanding was necessary in order to stay competitive.

In her late 60s, Carrie learned she had lung cancer. She would live several months with the disease, and she even continued to travel. But on one trip to New York she contracted pleurisy. She never recovered and died at her home at the age of 69, on Friday, March 6, 1953.

Carrie's obituary appeared in *The New York Times* two days later, under the headline "Mrs. Neiman Dead; Store Co-Founder." Below that was the subhead "Chairman of Neiman-Marcus in Dallas Started Business in '07 With Husband and Brother." With a dateline of Dallas, Texas, March 7, the obituary read:

Mrs. Carrie Neiman, world traveler, fashion authority and a co-founder of Dallas' Neiman-Marcus specialty store, died late last night at her home at the age of 69. She had been ill with pleurisy, contracted on a recent trip to New York.

At her death she was board chairman of Neiman-Marcus, a store whose reputation she helped build to national prominence.

Born in Louisville, Ky., Mrs. Neiman moved to Hillsboro, Tex., in 1895. Four years later she came to Dallas. She had devoted most of her time and efforts in the store since its founding in 1907.

Mrs. Neiman was well-known in American and European fashion capitals.

Started Store in Panic Year

Mrs. Neiman and her husband, A. L. Neiman[,] and her brother, Herbert Marcus Sr., founded the Dallas store in 1907, a panic year, with a then-radical policy of selling ready-made clothes to women. The enterprise was launched with a double-page ad in the

Dallas newspapers, proclaiming the store as a fashion center for Southern women.

How well the store succeeded is evidenced by the luxury merchandise, with price tickets in the thousands, that it now stocks. The Neiman-Marcus label has become internationally famous, and the company's representatives scour the markets of the world for new creations in the field of fashion. From a working capital of $50,000, the concern has grown to a multi-million-dollar business with stock market listing.

In 1928 Mr. Marcus purchased Mr. Neiman's interest but Mrs. Neiman remained active in the organization.

For the last fifteen years, Neiman-Marcus has held annual fall fashion expositions, at which leading figures in the field are presented with plaques for "distinguished service." The awards have gone to actresses, designers and other notable women, and to newspapers. In 1948 a Neiman-Marcus award was presented to *The New York Times*.

Page 158. Portrait of Carrie Marcus Neiman. 1951. Dallas.
Photographer unknown.

Masterful Design and Carrie's Extraordinary Taste

Carrie's funeral was held on a Sunday, two days after she died. The following day, both Neiman Marcus stores were closed all day in her memory, a fact that the family placed in a full-page advertisement in Dallas newspapers. The ad stated: "In Memoriam: Carrie Marcus Neiman, distinguished and beloved co-founder and Chairman of the Board, Neiman Marcus. Both Neiman Marcus stores will be closed today."

Carrie is buried near several family members, including her parents, at the Marcus plot at Temple Emanu-El Cemetery on the northern edge of downtown Dallas. Herbert and his wife, Minnie, are buried in a mausoleum at Sparkman

Hillcrest Memorial Park Cemetery in North Dallas, fittingly adjacent to the Neiman Marcus NorthPark Store.

Seven months after Carrie's death, her family established the Carrie Marcus Neiman Fashion Foundation. The foundation, a memorial to Carrie at the downtown Store, was made up of important clothing of Carrie's as well as photographs and drawings of fine apparel and accessories. A newspaper article about the foundation stated that the Marcus family wanted it to be available for use by students, writers, artists and designers "seeking authoritative historical fashion research." Seven years later, in 1960, those items became part of the Dallas Fashion Museum, which was housed not far from the Store, in Dallas's Merchandise Mart, at the corner of Ervay and Young streets.

The nucleus of the Fashion Museum was Carrie's personal wardrobe as well as gifts from her that her friends had received, kept through the years and donated to the museum. An article in one of the Dallas newspapers stated:

> It was the foresight of Stanley Marcus, who felt the need for a fashion museum in Dallas, that resulted in saving certain outstanding garments, which represented the look of a particular year. (Mrs. Neiman's) exquisite taste and knowledge of good design are apparent in the selections. Typical is a black velvet evening coat with sleeves of white ermine which Mrs. Neiman wore to grand occasions in the late 1920s.

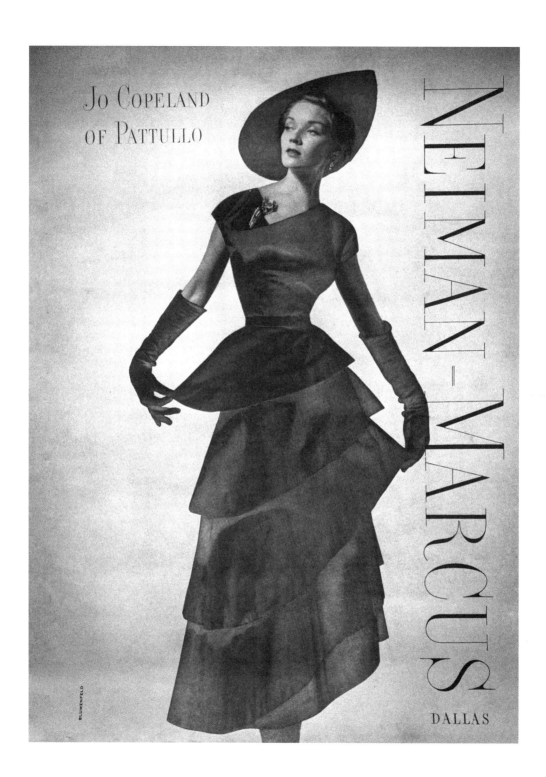

The fashion collection moved again, and today some 200 pieces of Carrie's apparel and other belongings are part of the Texas Fashion Collection at the University of North Texas in Denton. Students, online or in person, can learn firsthand about masterful design and Carrie's extraordinary taste as well as the tastes and styles of many other donors who have contributed more than 18,000 fashion items to the collection.

Carrie's legacy, of course, extended to her close-knit family. For a single woman in 1953, Carrie left behind a substantial estate that would continue to benefit her family for several decades. Among the bequests in her will, signed two years before her death, were generous trusts for her nieces and nephews that would pay their college tuition and other large expenses, just as she had done when she was alive. She also left gifts to her longtime housekeeper, Peachie Isaacs, as well as to Temple Emanu-El Cemetery and six charitable institutions.

In 1957, four years after Carrie died, the Store's advertising director Zula McCauley reflected on Carrie's life in a published history of the Store's first half-century:

It was an affectionate title — Mrs. Neiman — and an institutional one, for in a deeply personal sense and for many, she *was* Neiman Marcus. When ... Carrie Marcus Neiman[,] beloved co-founder and Chairman of the Board[,] died, much passed with her of the intimate memories of store beginnings and early struggles and success won under difficulties. ... In her quiet, patrician way she was, quite simply, a power — felt and accepted without explanation. She had the deep respect — more, the love — of those who knew her, co-workers and customers alike. As long as she was able it was Mrs. Neiman's joy to serve a few long-time customers who depended upon her unerring taste and her ability always to find "the right thing." To Mrs. Neiman, then, great lady and gentle wit, whose counsel and understanding was a cherished part of our lives.

Page 162. Carrie Marcus Neiman headstone at the Temple Emanu-El Cemetery in Dallas, Texas. Photograph by Allison V. Smith.

Page 165. Jo Copeland of Patullo Neiman Marcus women's dress, 1949 photograph by Erwin Blumenfeld.

CHAPTER FIFTEEN

She Was Born with "It"

As a teenager I had no lingering interest in the history of my great aunt Carrie, but as an adult I came to appreciate her for all of her extraordinary qualities. To this day, I have not known any woman or man with as much innate style and elegance. She was born with "it" — that sparkling, elusive quality that only the lucky few have and that everyone in the fashion business still dreams of. There will never be another Carrie Marcus Neiman, though there have been many who have tried (and will continue to try) to imitate her.

Carrie exuded shimmering vitality — whether she was wrapped in unapologetically luxurious Chinese silks or donning supple leathers that carried her through warm Texas autumns or showcasing the understated, classically elegant yet simple French fabrics that had launched her career. As Carrie aged, she retained that sophisticated air that I had mistaken, as an adolescent, for frostiness. In fact, her apparently severe air was actually an enormous dignity and poise other folks often lacked — an old-world elegance that she wore so easily and never shed in her later years, even when wearing her dressing gown and slippers.

Simply put, her kind has not been seen since.

Page 168. Carrie Marcus Neiman. 1951. Dallas. Photograph courtesy Neiman Marcus.

Page 171. Jerrie Marcus Smith. 2004. Dallas. Photograph by Allison V. Smith.

Image Credits

2-3, Thomas Benton Hollyman.

4-5, 18, 105, 110-111, 112, 116, 144-145, 154-155, John Rogers and Georgette de Bruchard Collection, University of North Texas Special Collections.

10, 109, Nina Leen/ The LIFE Picture Collection via Getty Images.

14-15, Rex Hardy Jr. Fortune Magazine. 1937.

16-17, Neiman Marcus Department Store.

34, 47, 48, 62-63, 71, 83, 92-93, 114-115, 140, 143, 146, 151, 152, DeGolyer Library, Southern Methodist University, Stanley Marcus Papers Collection.

42, Newspaper.com.

58-59, 80-81, 157, 158, From the collections of the Dallas History & Archives Division, Dallas Public Library.

95, NBC 5/KXAS Television News Collection, University of North Texas Special Collections.

121, Alfred Eisenstaedt/ The LIFE Picture Collection via Getty Images.

165, Neiman-Marcus ad for Jo Copeland. Photograph by Erwin Blumenfeld.

178-179, John Dominis/The LIFE Picture Collection via Getty Images.

184, Alfred Eisenstaedt/The LIFE Picture Collection/Shutterstock.

All other photographs provided by the Carrie Marcus Neiman Family.

Page 172. The author, Jerrie Marcus Smith, with her father, Stanley Marcus, before attending The Hockaday School's annual Dad's Dinner. Photograph by Billie Marcus.

Page 174-175. Family and friends sit on the walkway in front of Carrie's home on Swiss Avenue. (left to right) Carrie's sister Minnie Rosenbaum, Roberta Miller, Lawrence Miller Jr., Abe and Rosalie Rosenbaum, Rhea Miller, Carrie Neiman, Herbert Sondheim, and Dave Leonard.

Page 176. Wendy, Billie and Jerrie Marcus photographed in their backyard. Photograph by Elsbeth Juda, 1947.

Page 177. Stanley and Jerrie Marcus photographed at home, 1937.

Page 178-179. Carrie Neiman sits front-row at a Neiman-Marcus fashion show. Photograph by John Dominis.

Page 180-183. Post war letter from Carrie Neiman to her family from a buying trip in London, England.

Page 184. Model wearing clothes by designer Hattie Carnegie for a show at Neiman-Marcus in downtown Dallas. October 1939. Photograph by Alfred Eisenstaedt.

CLARIDGE'S LONDON

TELEPHONE, MAYFAIR 8860   TELEGRAMS, CLARIDGES LONDON

Dearest Ones   Tuesday —
1. We were delighted
to have such interesting mail
from you today. Your trip to
Colorado sounded glamorous.
Well in all my life I have
never seen such darling
people as the Judás'. they have
been marvelous to us. I am
afraid to mention anything
we would like to do around
there, for no sooner said
than they do it.
We are finding London most

interesting and could
spend much more time
here than planned, but
we leave here Wed. nite for
Holland –

Today I went to Hartnel
and Hardy Amies, they
have nothing new that is
the lines will not be
shown until July 25th.
I am considering and
will probably buy one
evening dress at Hartnels.
Hardy Amies is very excited
over an order that he has
taken for Princess Elizabeth
those numbers are not
to be shown to anyone

CLARIDGE'S LONDON

TELEPHONE, MAYFAIR 8860   TELEGRAMS, CLARIDGES LONDON

he said. She bought 8 peices
So we saw nothing but
a few suits. I wrote one
number. Elsbeth took us
to Jackmar and I like two
suit numbers there designed
by Digby Morton that laind
at $80 00 So will probably buy
four or five peices in plaids.
Also went to house by the
name of Stork. Elsbeth says
it is the best cheap line
here but I did not like it.
So the purchases here will

her light. We were delighted
to hear Nancy is coming
with Laurie,   ④
I Know Minnie writes in
Detail of our doings, and
I will say we have been
on a merry chase —
We had dinner tonite
after theatre at the Savoy, I
still like it best of all
hotels here —
     Gots of love to all, it
is very late so will sign
off,
          Devotedly
          Aunt Carrie,
The Childrens letters here
from darling,